Table of Contents

Meet the...

How to Use This Book

The ability to recognize word family patterns is an important part of learning to read. The stories and activities in this book help students increase their reading vocabulary while practicing the essential phonological skills of onset and rime. Each unit follows a consistent format:

Introduce the Word Family

Model blending each initial sound with the word family phoneme. Ask students to point to each picture as they repeat the word after you. Then have students follow the directions to complete the page.

Read the Story

Instruct students to follow along as you read the story aloud. Then have students underline each word family word in the story or poem. Have students read the story again using one of the following methods:

- Read silently
- Echo read
- Choral read

Complete the Activity Pages

The activity pages after each story practice the word family presented and follow a consistent format, leading students to work independently.

Use the Slider

The slider is a quick and easy tool that encourages repeated practice of word family vocabulary, leading to increased oral reading fluency.

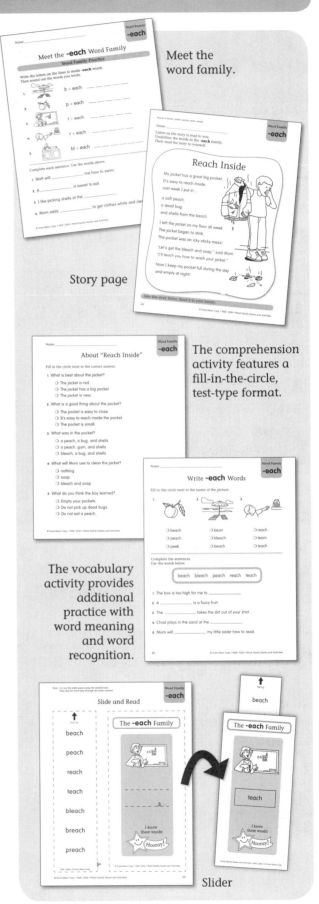

Meet the word family.

Story page

The comprehension activity features a fill-in-the-circle, test-type format.

The vocabulary activity provides additional practice with word meaning and word recognition.

Slider

Meet the **-ain** Word Family

Word Family Practice

Write the letters on the lines to make **-ain** words.
Then sound out the words you wrote.

1.    st + ain   __ __ __ __ __

2.   br + ain   __ __ __ __ __

3.    dr + ain   __ __ __ __ __

4.    str + ain   __ __ __ __ __ __

Read these **-ain** words.

main   pain   plain

Complete each sentence. Use the words above.

1. Some eggs are _____ and some eggs have spots.

2. The stores are on the _____ street in town.

3. The water goes down the _____.

Words to know: elf, searched, spines, hooted
Teacher: Read the story to your students.

Word Family
-ain

Name _____

Listen as the story is read to you.
Underline the words in the **-ain** family.
Then read the story to yourself.

A Home for Owl

An elf owl searched for a home.

She stopped by a plant that was as tall as a tree.

"Living here could be a strain.

This home has only one main room.

It is very plain," she said.

"But the thick walls will keep out the rain.

I hope the sharp spines will not be a pain.

"I'll have to think about it."

Owl used her tiny brain.

"I'll take it!" she hooted.

Take the story home. Read it to your family.

4   Word Family Stories and Activities • EMC 3356 • © Evan-Moor Corp.

About "A Home for Owl"

Fill in the circle next to the correct answer.

1. What is the story about?

○ Owl lays eggs.
○ Owl needs food.
○ Owl looks for a home.

2. What will the thick walls keep out?

○ the owl
○ the rain
○ the sharp spines

3. Where do you think Owl's home is?

○ in a tree
○ in a nest
○ in a cactus

Check all that tell about Owl's home.

_____ a big roof   _____ very plain

_____ thick walls   _____ sharp spines

_____ one main room   _____ as short as a bush

Name_____

Write **-ain** Words

Write the name of each picture.

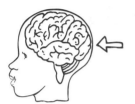  

1. _____   2. _____   3. _____

Complete the sentences. Use the words below.

gain   main   pain   rain   brain   train

1. When I run, I get a sharp _____ in my side.

2. The _____ fell onto the land.

3. What is the name of the _____ street in your town?

4. The _____ pulled 100 cars.

5. A baby will _____ weight quickly.

6. Your _____ helps you learn.

   Word Family Stories and Activities • EMC 3356 • © Evan-Moor Corp.

Note: Cut out the slider parts along the dashed lines.
Then slip the word strip through the slider window.

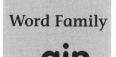

Word Family

-ain

Slide and Read

↑

Pull Up

gain

main

pain

rain

brain

chain

drain

plain

stain

strain

train

The **-ain** Family

I know
these words!

Hooray!

EMC 3356 • © Evan-Moor Corp.

Word Family Stories and Activities • EMC 3356 • © Evan-Moor Corp.

gain

main

rain

brain

pain

pain

end of
-ain family

chain

drain

brain

gain

plain

stain

rain

train

main

Name _____

Meet the **-are** Word Family

Word Family Practice

Write the letters on the lines to make -**are** words.
Then sound out the words you wrote.

1.   c + are   ___ ___ ___ ___

2.    h + are   ___ ___ ___ ___

3.    sc + are   ___ ___ ___ ___ ___

4.    sh + are   ___ ___ ___ ___ ___

5.   st + are   ___ ___ ___ ___ ___

Read these -**are** words.

bare   dare   mare

Complete each sentence. Use the words above.

1. The big dog's bark gave me a _____!

2. A rabbit and a _____ are alike in some ways.

3. Clare will _____ her cookies with you.

Words to know: grew, carrots, together, knew, raced, yelled
Teacher: Read the story to your students.

Name_____

Listen as the story is read to you.
Underline the words in the **-are** family.
Then read the story to yourself.

The Dare

Crab and Hare grew carrots together.

But Hare did not care to share any of

the carrots. He wanted to eat them all.

Crab knew that Hare did not want to share.

So he came up with a plan. He said,

"Hare, I dare you to race me to the carrot pile!

The first one to get there wins all the carrots."

Hare knew that Crab was slow. So Hare took the dare.

He raced toward the carrot pile so fast that he did not feel

Crab grab onto his tail.

Once he reached it, Crab let go of Hare's

tail and landed on top of the pile.

"I win!" yelled Crab.

He gave Hare quite a scare.

All Hare could do was stare.

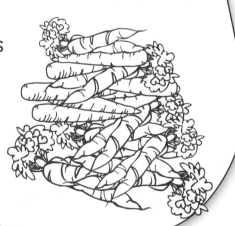

Take the story home. Read it to your family.

Word Family Stories and Activities • EMC 3356 • © Evan-Moor Corp.

About "The Dare"

Circle one sentence in Beginning, Middle, and End to retell the story.

Beginning	Middle	End
1. Hare won't share the carrots.	1. Crab and Hare grow carrots.	1. Crab and Hare eat carrots.
2. Crab won't share the carrots.	2. Crab wins the carrots.	2. Crab wins the carrots.
3. Hare races fast.	3. Crab dares Hare to race.	3. Hare wins the carrots.

Fill in the circle next to the correct answer.

1. What do Crab and Hare do together?

   ○ grow carrots

   ○ win carrots

   ○ win dares

2. Which one tells about Crab?

   ○ Crab is fast.

   ○ Crab is smart.

   ○ Crab does not like to share.

3. What is another good title for the story?

   ○ Carrots Are Good

   ○ Hare Races Fast

   ○ Crab Tricks Hare

Name_____

Write **-are** Words

Complete the sentences.
Use the words below.

| dare | mare | scare | share | stare |

1. That loud noise gave us a _____.

2. My brother and I _____ a bedroom.

3. My dad does not _____ speed when he drives.

4. I tried not to _____ at Clare's green hair.

5. A girl horse is called a _____.

Fill in the circle next to the name of the picture.

1.

○ have

○ hear

○ hare

2.

○ more

○ mare

○ dare

3.

○ scare

○ stare

○ square

Note: Cut out the slider parts along the dashed lines.
Then slip the word strip through the slider window.

Slide and Read

↑
Pull Up

bare

care

dare

hare

mare

rare

aware

scare

share

stare

square

The **-are** Family

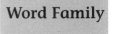

I know
these words!

Hooray!

Word Family Stories and Activities • EMC 3356 • © Evan-Moor Corp.

EMC 3356 • © Evan-Moor Corp.

bare

dare

care

hare

mare

rare

end of
-are family

aware

scare

share

hare

care

stare

mare

square

rare

Name _____

Meet the **-aw** Word Family

Word Family Practice

Write the letters on the lines to make **-aw** words.
Then sound out the words you wrote.

1.   j + aw   ___ ___ ___

2.   p + aw   ___ ___ ___

3.   r + aw   ___ ___ ___

4. 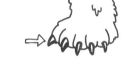   cl + aw   ___ ___ ___ ___

5.    gn + aw   ___ ___ ___ ___

6.   str + aw   ___ ___ ___ ___ ___

Complete each sentence. Use the words above.

1. Polar bears eat _____ meat.

2. The bear will _____ on the bone until it is eaten.

3. Each _____ is sharp and pointed.

Words to know: icy, polar, seems
Teacher: Read the story to your students.

Word Family

-aw

Name _____

Listen as the story is read to you.
Underline the words in the **-aw** family.
Then read the story to yourself.

Claws and Paws

How can a polar bear live on ice?

A polar bear has two coats of white fur.

One thick coat keeps the bear warm.

Another coat stands up like straws.

That fur keeps the bear dry.

A bear's paws have claws.

Each claw works like a hook.

Claws help the bear climb and dig.

A polar bear needs a lot of food.

Its jaw is strong to catch raw meat.

Its teeth are long to gnaw on bones.

An icy home seems just right for a polar bear!

Take the story home. Read it to your family.

Word Family Stories and Activities • EMC 3356 • © Evan-Moor Corp.

About "Claws and Paws"

How can a polar bear live on ice?
Draw lines to show.

1. A bear has thick fur   •   • to keep dry.

2. A bear has fur like straws   •   • to climb on ice.

3. A bear has claws   •   • to gnaw on bones.

4. A bear has long teeth   •   • to keep warm.

Fill in the circle next to the correct answer.

1. A polar bear lives where it is very hot.

    ○ yes
    ○ no

2. A polar bear has paws with claws.

    ○ yes
    ○ no

3. A polar bear has two coats of white fur.

    ○ yes
    ○ no

4. A polar bear's jaw is made for eating leaves.

    ○ yes
    ○ no

Name_____

Write **-aw** Words

Write the name of each picture.

1. _____   2. _____   3. _____

Complete the sentences. Use the words below.

claw   draw   law   paw   raw

1. I like to _____ pictures of my family.

2. A dog's foot is called a _____.

3. A cat's nail is called a _____.

4. Meat is _____ when it is not cooked.

5. Do not break the _____.

Use the word **straw** in a sentence.

_____

_____

Slide and Read

↑

Pull Up

jaw

law

paw

raw

saw

claw

draw

flaw

gnaw

straw

The -aw Family

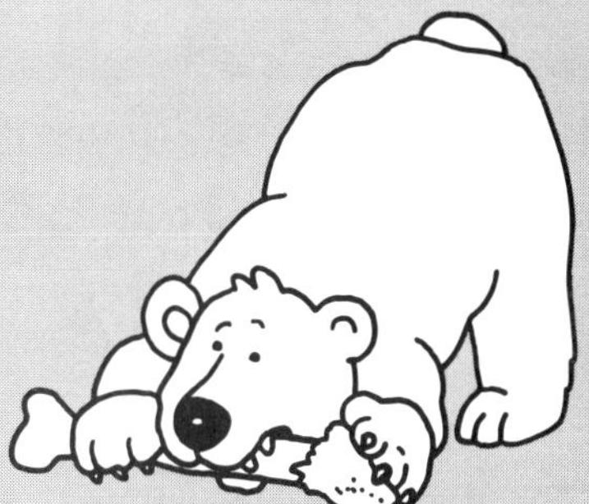

I know
these words!

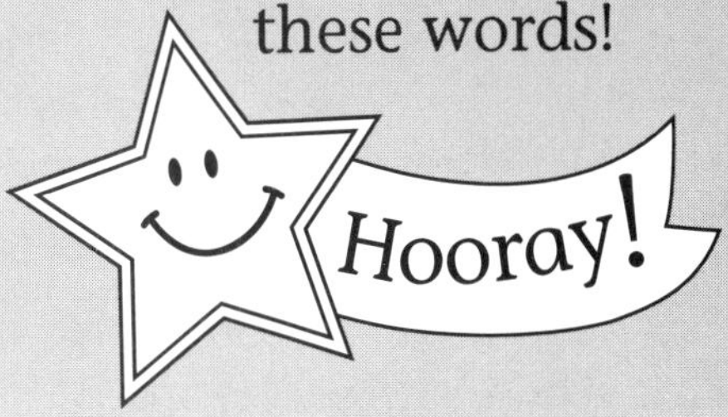

Hooray!

paw

jaw

law

raw

saw

claw

end of
-aw family

draw

claw

flaw

law

gnaw

paw

jaw

straw

draw

Meet the -each Word Family

Word Family Practice

Write the letters on the lines to make -each words.
Then sound out the words you wrote.

1.    b + each   ___ ___ ___ ___ ___

2.    p + each   ___ ___ ___ ___ ___

3.    t + each   ___ ___ ___ ___ ___

4.    r + each   ___ ___ ___ ___ ___

5.    bl + each   ___ ___ ___ ___ ___ ___

Complete each sentence. Use the words above.

1. Matt will _____ me how to swim.

2. A _____ is sweet to eat.

3. I like picking shells at the _____.

4. Mom adds _____ to get clothes white and clean.

Words to know: jacket, pocket, stink, empty
Teacher: Read the story to your students.

Word Family
-each

Name_____

Listen as the story is read to you.
Underline the words in the **-each** family.
Then read the story to yourself.

Reach Inside

My jacket has a great big pocket.

It's easy to reach inside.

Last week I put in…

a soft peach,

a dead bug,

and shells from the beach.

I left the jacket on my floor all week.

The jacket began to stink.

The pocket was an icky-sticky mess!

"Let's get the bleach and soap," said Mom.

"I'll teach you how to wash your jacket."

Now I keep my pocket full during the day

and empty at night!

Take the story home. Read it to your family.

22
Word Family Stories and Activities • EMC 3356 • © Evan-Moor Corp.

Name _____

About "Reach Inside"

Fill in the circle next to the correct answer.

1. What is best about the jacket?

   ○ The jacket is red.
   ○ The jacket has a big pocket.
   ○ The jacket is new.

2. What is a good thing about the pocket?

   ○ The pocket is easy to close.
   ○ It's easy to reach inside the pocket.
   ○ The pocket is small.

3. What was in the pocket?

   ○ a peach, a bug, and shells
   ○ a peach, gum, and shells
   ○ bleach, a bug, and shells

4. What will Mom use to clean the jacket?

   ○ nothing
   ○ soap
   ○ bleach and soap

5. What do you think the boy learned?

   ○ Empty your pockets.
   ○ Do not pick up dead bugs.
   ○ Do not eat a peach.

Write -each Words

Fill in the circle next to the name of the picture.

1.

   ○ beach

   ○ peach

   ○ peek

2.

   ○ bean

   ○ bleach

   ○ beach

3.

   ○ reach

   ○ team

   ○ teach

Complete the sentences.
Use the words below.

| beach | bleach | peach | reach | teach |

1. The box is too high for me to _____.

2. A _____ is a fuzzy fruit.

3. The _____ takes the dirt out of your shirt.

4. Chad plays in the sand at the _____.

5. Mom will _____ my little sister how to read.

Note: Cut out the slider parts along the dashed lines.
Then slip the word strip through the slider window.

Slide and Read

↑
Pull Up

beach

peach

reach

teach

bleach

breach

preach

The **-each** Family

I know
these words!

Hooray!

beach

peach

reach

teach

bleach

reach

end of
-**each** family

breach

beach

teach

bleach

preach

peach

reach

breach

beach

Name _____

Meet the -ew Word Family

Word Family Practice

Write the letters on the lines to make -**ew** words.
Then sound out the words you made.

1.   d + ew   ___ ___ ___

2.   ch + ew   ___ ___ ___ ___

3.   fl + ew   ___ ___ ___ ___

4.   gr + ew   ___ ___ ___ ___

5.   st + ew   ___ ___ ___ ___

Read these -**ew** words.

few   new   threw

Complete each sentence. Use the words above.

1. Dad put meat and lots of carrots in the _____.

2. There were drops of _____ on the grass this morning.

3. The bugs _____ near the light.

Words to know: pretend, watched, feather, horn
Teacher: Read the story to your students.

Word Family

-ew

Name _____

Listen as the story is read to you.
Underline the words in the **-ew** family.
Then read the story to yourself.

A Silly Stew

My sister Lily likes to pretend she's a cook.

I watched Lily make a stew for her dolls.

Into a pot Lily threw…

a feather that flew,

a few nuts to chew,

grass that once grew,

some drops of dew,

a toy horn that blew,

two nails and a screw,

and a dime that was new.

Ew!

I'm glad that stew's not for me!

Word Family Stories and Activities • EMC 3356 • © Evan-Moor Corp.

Name _____

Word Family
-ew

About "A Silly Stew"

Fill in the circle next to the correct answer.

1. Who?

○ my friend Lily
○ my mom
○ my sister Lily

2. What?

○ eats a stew
○ makes a stew
○ fries a stew

3. Why?

○ Lily is a cook.
○ Lily pretends to cook for her dolls.
○ Lily is little.

Draw lines to match. Show what was in the stew.

1. a toy horn •   • that was new

2. nuts •   • that blew

3. a dime •   • that once grew

4. grass •   • to chew

© Evan-Moor Corp. • EMC 3356 • Word Family Stories and Activities

29

Name _____

Write -ew Words

Complete the sentences.
Use the words below.

> blew   flew   grew   knew   threw

1. Ava _____ a bubble with her gum.

2. Mom _____ the beach ball to Ryan.

3. The bird _____ up to its nest in the tree.

4. I _____ how to spell all the words on the test.

5. The seeds _____ into a flower.

Add other things to Lily's stew.
Fill in the blanks with your ideas.

1. a _____ that once grew

2. a _____ to chew

3. a _____ that was new

Note: Cut out the slider parts along the dashed lines.
Then slip the word strip through the slider window.

Slide and Read

↑
Pull Up

dew

few

new

blew

chew

flew

grew

knew

stew

screw

threw

The **-ew** Family

I know
these words!

Hooray!

Word Family Stories and Activities • EMC 3356 • © Evan-Moor Corp.

dew

few

threw

grew

blew

new

end of
-ew family

screw

dew

blew

new

stew

chew

knew

flew

threw

Name_____

Meet the **-ead** Word Family

Word Family Practice

Write the letters on the lines to make -**ead** words.
Then sound out the words you wrote.

1.   h + ead ___ ___ ___ ___

2.   r + ead ___ ___ ___ ___

3.   br + ead ___ ___ ___ ___ ___

4.   spr + ead ___ ___ ___ ___ ___ ___

5.   thr + ead ___ ___ ___ ___ ___ ___

Read these -**ead** words.

dead   lead   dread

Complete each sentence. Use the words above.

1. I _____ that book last year.

2. Mom will sew the dress with red _____.

3. Evan _____ a lot of peanut butter on the bread.

Words to know: peanut butter, pretend, raisins, cheese, banana
Teacher: Read the story to your students.

Name _____

Listen as the story is read to you.
Underline the words in the **-ead** family.
Then read the story to yourself.

Food Face

I read this idea in a cookbook for kids.

It is called "Food Face." Here's how it goes:

You can make your face and eat it, too.

First, take one slice of bread.

Then, spread it with peanut butter.

Pretend that the bread is a head.

Make eyes with raisins.

Make a smile with jam.

Pull cheese into strings as thin as thread.

Use the strings to shape hair.

Cut the tip of a banana to form a nose.

Now go ahead and eat your face.

You will taste good!

Take the story home. Read it to your family.

 Word Family Stories and Activities • EMC 3356 • © Evan-Moor Corp.

Name_____

About "Food Face"

Fill in the circle next to the correct answer.

1. Where did the food face idea come from?

   ○ It was read in school.

   ○ It was read in a funny book.

   ○ It was read in a cookbook for kids.

2. What is spread on the bread?

   ○ butter

   ○ peanut butter

   ○ jam

3. What do you pretend about the bread?

   ○ The bread is a head.

   ○ The bread is a bed.

   ○ The bread is a sled.

4. What do you make with strings of cheese?

   ○ big eyes

   ○ hair on the head

   ○ thin thread

5. What is the last thing you do?

   ○ use strings to shape hair

   ○ make eyes with raisins

   ○ eat your face

Write -ead Words

Complete the sentences.
Use the words below.

> bread   head   lead   spread   thread

1. The cap does not fit Luke's _____.

2. The pipe in the sink is made of _____.

3. I need _____ to sew on the button.

4. I can smell the _____ baking in the oven.

5. I like to _____ butter on crackers.

Fill in the circle next to the name of the picture.

1.

○ brain

○ dead

○ bread

2.

○ heat

○ head

○ read

3.

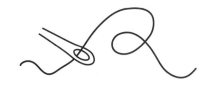

○ thread

○ tread

○ spread

Note: Cut out the slider parts along the dashed lines.
      Then slip the word strip through the slider window.

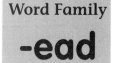

Word Family

-ead

Slide and Read

↑

Pull Up

dead

head

lead

read

ahead

bread

dread

spread

thread

The -ead Family

I know
these words!

Hooray!

dead

head

read

ahead

lead

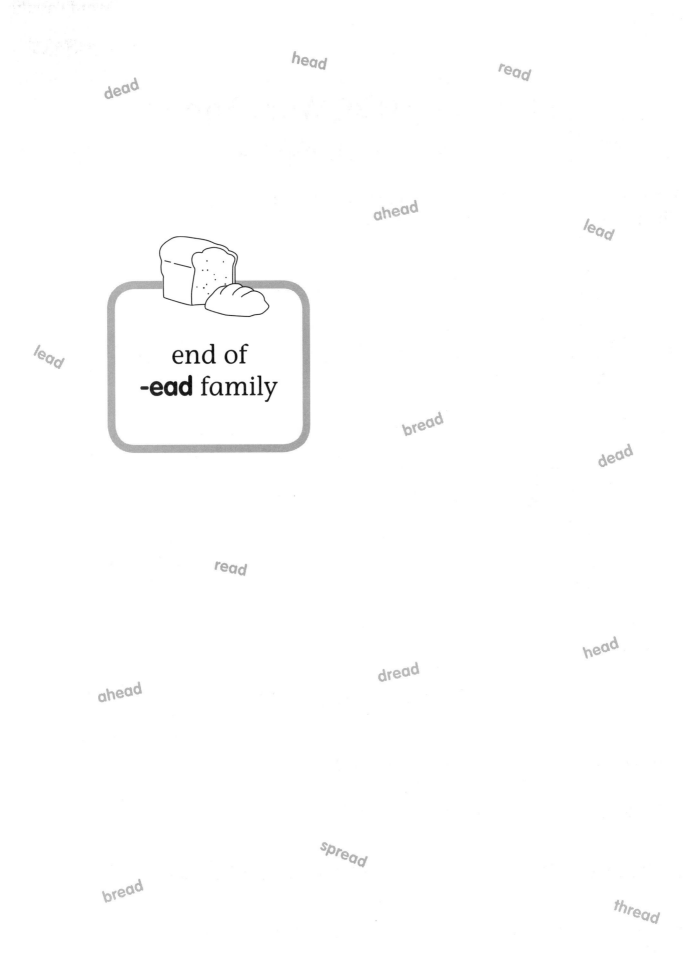

lead

end of
-ead family

bread

dead

read

head

dread

ahead

spread

bread

thread

Name_____

Meet the **-ear** Word Family

Word Family Practice

Write the letters on the lines to make -**ear** words.
Then sound out the words you wrote.

1.    d + ear   ___ ___ ___ ___

2.    g + ear   ___ ___ ___ ___

3.   h + ear   ___ ___ ___ ___

4.   y + ear   ___ ___ ___ ___

5.   cl + ear   ___ ___ ___ ___ ___

Read these -**ear** words.

fear   hear   tear

Complete each sentence. Use the words above.

1. I will be seven years old this _____.

2. The lake is so _____, I can see a lot of fish.

3. The only camping _____ I have is a tent.

Name _____

Listen as the story is read to you.
Underline the words in the **-ear** family.
Then read the story to yourself.

Camping at Clear Lake

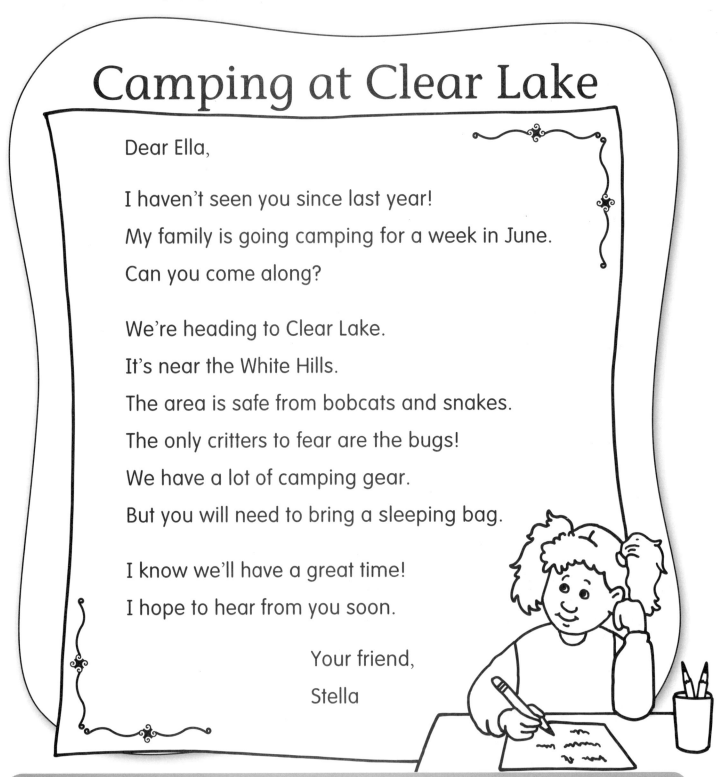

Dear Ella,

I haven't seen you since last year!

My family is going camping for a week in June.

Can you come along?

We're heading to Clear Lake.

It's near the White Hills.

The area is safe from bobcats and snakes.

The only critters to fear are the bugs!

We have a lot of camping gear.

But you will need to bring a sleeping bag.

I know we'll have a great time!

I hope to hear from you soon.

Your friend,

Stella

Take the story home. Read it to your family.

Name _____

About "Camping at Clear Lake"

Fill in the circle next to the correct answer.

1. Stella and Ella know each other.

   ○ yes   ○ no

2. Ella is inviting Stella to go camping.

   ○ yes   ○ no

3. Ella needs to bring a lot of camping gear.

   ○ yes   ○ no

4. Ella and Stella should bring bug spray.

   ○ yes   ○ no

5. Bobcats live around Clear Lake.

   ○ yes   ○ no

6. Clear Lake is near the Red Hills.

   ○ yes   ○ no

7. Critters probably means "animals."

   ○ yes   ○ no

8. Stella's family is going camping in July.

   ○ yes   ○ no

Name_____

Write -ear Words

Write the name of each picture.

1. _____ 2. _____ 3. _____

Complete the sentences.
Use the words below.

> fear hear near clear smear

1. Jake lives _____ his grandma.

2. Some people have a _____ of spiders.

3. The night sky was _____, so I saw lots of stars.

4. Let the paint dry or it will _____.

5. I could _____ the rain hit the roof.

Word Family Stories and Activities • EMC 3356 • © Evan-Moor Corp.

Note: Cut out the slider parts along the dashed lines.
Then slip the word strip through the slider window.

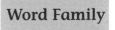

Slide and Read

↑
Pull Up

dear

fear

gear

hear

near

rear

tear

year

clear

smear

spear

The **-ear** Family

I know
these words!

Hooray!

dear

fear

near

spear

gear

gear

end of
-**ear** family

rear

dear

near

fear

year

tear

smear

clear

hear

Name _____

Meet the **-ight** Word Family

Word Family Practice

Write the letters on the lines to make **-ight** words.
Then sound out the words you made.

1.    f + ight   ___ ___ ___ ___ ___

2.    l + ight   ___ ___ ___ ___

3.    n + ight   ___ ___ ___ ___ ___

4.    r + ight   ___ ___ ___ ___

5.   br + ight   ___ ___ ___ ___ ___ ___

Read these **-ight** words.

might   sight   tight

Complete each sentence. Use the words above.

1. The _____ light hurt my eyes.

2. My shoes are too _____.

3. Turn on the _____ when you read.

Name _____

Listen as the story is read to you.
Underline the words in the **-ight** family.
Then read the story to yourself.

The Bright Light

It was late on a very dark night.

Juan and Carlos were camping out in a tent in the yard.

All of a sudden, Juan jumped in the darkness.

"Do you see that?" asked Juan.

"See what? That bright light?" asked Carlos.

"Yes, that bright light," said Juan.

"Yes, I see it. Don't let it give you a fright.

It is just Mr. Bretten. He has very poor sight.

He carries a flashlight when he walks his dog at night,"
said Carlos.

"Oh, yeah, right, Mr. Bretten.

Don't worry, it didn't give me a fright," said Juan.

"OK. Good night," said Carlos.

"Good night," said Juan.

Take the story home. Read it to your family.

Name _____

About "The Bright Light"

Fill in the circle next to the correct answer.

1. Who is the story about?

○ Mr. Bretten's dog

○ Juan and Carlos

○ neighbors

2. What makes the bright light?

○ Mr. Bretten's flashlight

○ the streetlight

○ Juan and Carlos's flashlight

3. Where were Juan and Carlos?

○ in the house

○ in a car

○ in a tent

4. What was Mr. Bretten doing?

○ taking out the garbage

○ walking his dog

○ looking for Juan and Carlos

5. What did Juan and Carlos say to each other at the end of the story?

○ good morning

○ good-bye

○ good night

Name_____

Write **-ight** Words

Complete the sentences.
Use the words below.

> fright   light   night   right   tight

1. "Good _____ and sleep tight," said Mom.

2. That bad dream gave me a _____.

3. I got bigger, and now my shirt is too _____.

4. The street_____ was broken.

5. Always try to do what is _____.

Write a sentence. Use the word **light** in your sentence.

_____

_____.

Write a sentence. Use the word **night** in your sentence.

_____

_____.

Word Family Stories and Activities • EMC 3356 • © Evan-Moor Corp.

Note: Cut out the slider parts along the dashed lines.
Then slip the word strip through the slider window.

Slide and Read

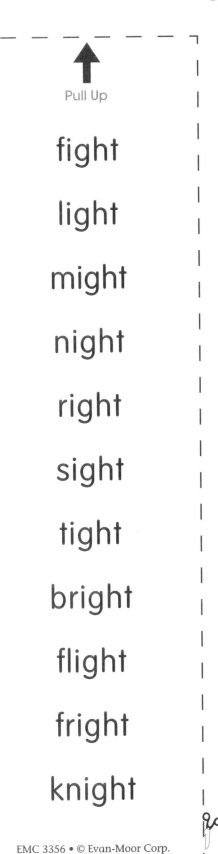

↑
Pull Up

fight

light

might

night

right

sight

tight

bright

flight

fright

knight

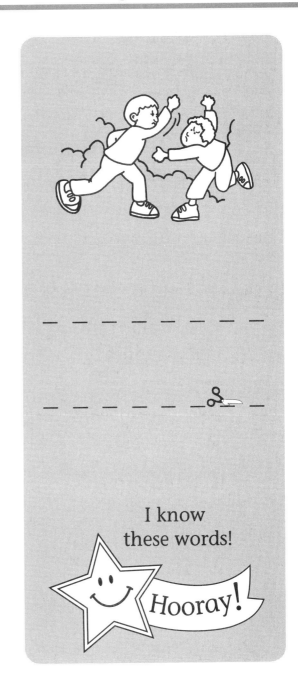

The **-ight** Family

I know
these words!

Hooray!

light

might

fight

right

night

night

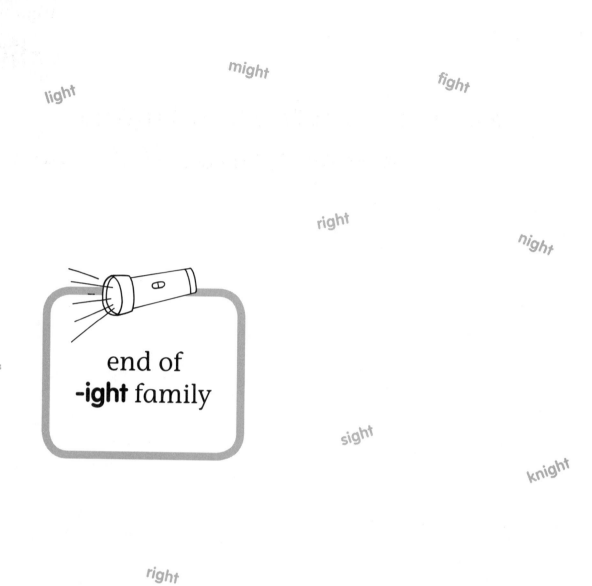

end of
-ight family

sight

knight

right

light

tight

fright

flight

bright

might

50

Name _____

Meet the -itch Word Family

Word Family Practice

Write the letters on the lines to make -itch words.
Then sound out the words you wrote.

1.    d + itch   __ __ __ __ __

2.    h + itch   __ __ __ __

3.   p + itch   __ __ __ __ __

4.    st + itch   __ __ __ __ __ __ __

Read these -itch words.

twitch   snitch   switch

Complete each sentence. Use the words above.

1. A rabbit can _____ its nose quickly.

2. My socks were coming down. I gave them a _____.

3. Mrs. Evans asked me to _____ seats with John.

Words to know: ready, plate, smack, slides
Teacher: Read the story to your students.

Word Family
-itch

Name_____

Listen as the story is read to you.
Underline the words in the **-itch** family.
Then read the story to yourself.

The First Pitch

It's Joy's turn to hit.

First, she stops to switch bats.

Then, she gives her pants a hitch.

She must be ready for the first pitch.

Joy steps to the plate.

Her arm gives a bit of a twitch.

Now she is ready for the first pitch.

Here it comes.

Smack! Wow!

Joy runs to first base, second base, and third.

She slides right into home plate.

Joy hit that first pitch just great!

Take the story home. Read it to your family.

Name_____

About "The First Pitch"

Fill in the circle next to the correct answer.

1. Who is the story about?
   - ○ a baseball team
   - ○ Joy
   - ○ a pitcher

2. What must Joy be ready for?
   - ○ the first pitch
   - ○ to give her pants a hitch
   - ○ to slide

3. Did Joy hit the first pitch?
   - ○ yes
   - ○ no

Draw a line to make a match.

1.  •   • Joy hit the first pitch.

2.  •   • Joy gives her pants a hitch.

3.  •   • Joy stops to switch bats.

Name_____

Write **-itch** Words

Fill in the circle next to the name of the picture.

1.

2.

3.

○ glitch	○ pit	○ switch
○ dirt	○ pitch	○ ditch
○ ditch	○ hitch	○ stitch

Complete the sentences.
Use the words below.

> ditch   pitch   stitch   switch   twitch

1. Ned will _____ the ball to the batter.

2. Mom uses thread to sew a _____.

3. Anna wants to _____ places with me in line.

4. The men dug a _____ for the pipe.

5. My cat will _____ her nose when she smells tuna.

Note: Cut out the slider parts along the dashed lines.
Then slip the word strip through the slider window.

Slide and Read

↑
Pull Up

ditch

hitch

pitch

glitch

snitch

stitch

switch

twitch

The **-itch** Family

I know
these words!

Hooray!

Word Family Stories and Activities • EMC 3356 • © Evan-Moor Corp.

ditch

hitch

snitch

glitch

stitch

pitch

end of
-itch family

switch

ditch

stitch

twitch

hitch

snitch

switch

glitch

pitch

Name _____

Meet the **-ook** Word Family

Word Family Practice

Write the letters on the lines to make **-ook** words.
Then sound out the words you made.

 1.  b + ook ___ ___ ___ ___

2. c + ook ___ ___ ___ ___

3. h + ook ___ ___ ___ ___

4. l + ook ___ ___ ___ ___

5.  t + ook ___ ___ ___ ___

6. sh + ook ___ ___ ___ ___ ___

Complete each sentence. Use the words above.

1. I hang my towel on a _____ by the tub.

2. The men _____ hands when they met.

3. The _____ made a pot of chicken stew.

Words to know: roared, pointed, shovels, trash
Teacher: Read the story to your students.

Word Family

-ook

Name _____

Listen as the story is read to you.
Underline the words in the **-ook** family.
Then read the story to yourself.

Pirate Pete

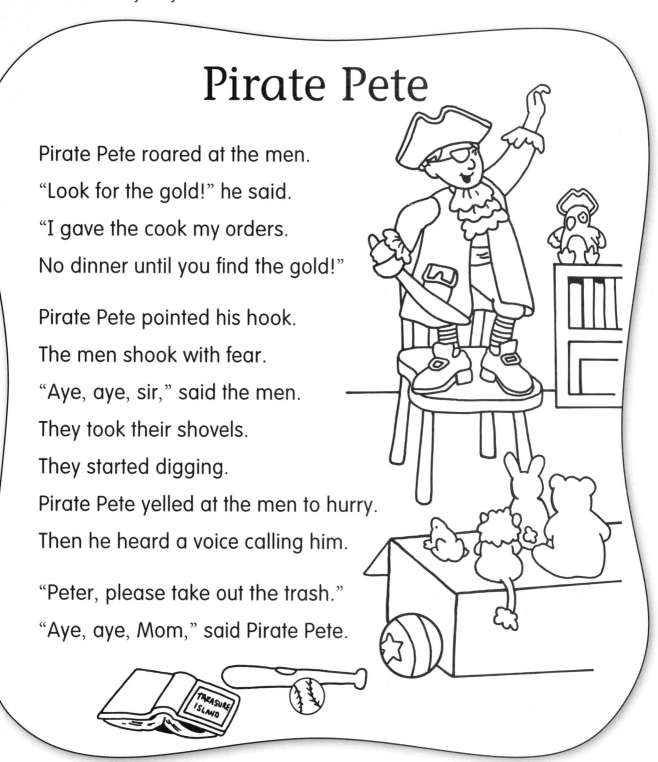

Pirate Pete roared at the men.

"Look for the gold!" he said.

"I gave the cook my orders.

No dinner until you find the gold!"

Pirate Pete pointed his hook.

The men shook with fear.

"Aye, aye, sir," said the men.

They took their shovels.

They started digging.

Pirate Pete yelled at the men to hurry.

Then he heard a voice calling him.

"Peter, please take out the trash."

"Aye, aye, Mom," said Pirate Pete.

Take the story home. Read it to your family.

About "Pirate Pete"

Fill in the circle next to the correct answer.

1. What is the story about?

   ○ Peter is a real pirate.

   ○ Peter will not help his mom.

   ○ Peter makes believe he's a pirate.

   ○ Pirate Pete has a hook.

2. When can the cook make the food?

   ○ at night

   ○ when Pirate Pete tells him to

   ○ when the men find the water

   ○ when the men find the gold

3. **Aye**, **aye** is a way to say, "_____."

   ○ No way

   ○ You do it

   ○ Yes

   ○ I'll do it later

4. Which word tells that Pirate Pete spoke loudly to the men?

   ○ said

   ○ roared

   ○ pointed

   ○ shook

Name _____

Write **-ook** Words

Write the name of each picture.

1. _____   2. _____   3. _____

Complete the sentences.
Use the words below.

book   brook   crook   hook   shook

1. Frogs live in the _____.

2. My cap hangs on a _____ in my room.

3. The _____ took money from the bank.

4. My hands _____ because I was very cold.

5. I like to read a _____ before I fall asleep.

Write a sentence about a story you read. Use the word **book** in your sentence.

_____

_____.

Word Family Stories and Activities • EMC 3356 • © Evan-Moor Corp.

Note: Cut out the slider parts along the dashed lines.
      Then slip the word strip through the slider window.

Slide and Read

↑
Pull Up

book

cook

hook

look

took

brook

crook

shook

overlook

unhook

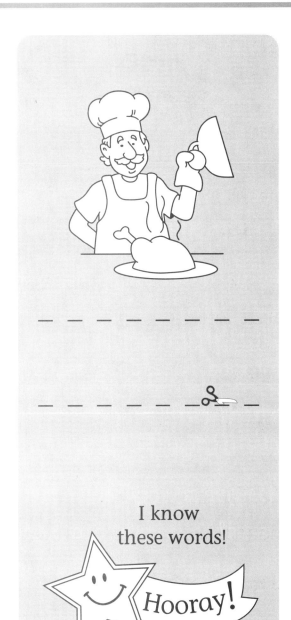

The **-ook** Family

I know
these words!

Hooray!

book look hook

brook took

hook

end of
-ook family

crook

cook

took

look

shook

brook

unhook

crook

overlook

Name _____

Meet the **-ool** Word Family

Word Family Practice

Write the letters on the lines to make **-ool** words.
Then sound out the words you made.

1.   c + ool   ___ ___ ___ ___

2.   p + ool   ___ ___ ___ ___

3.    t + ool   ___ ___ ___ ___

4.   dr + ool   ___ ___ ___ ___ ___

5.   sch + ool   ___ ___ ___ ___ ___ ___

Read these **-ool** words.

fool   spool   stool

Complete each sentence. Use the words above.

1. An otter uses a stone like a _____ to open a shell.

2. Some animals _____ when they're hungry.

3. A group of cows is called a herd. A group of fish is called

   a _____ .

Words to know: howls, curvy, purr
Teacher: Read the story to your students.

Name _____

Listen as the story is read to you.
Underline the words in the **-ool** family.
Then read the story to yourself.

Who's Who at the Zoo?

Who did we see at the zoo?
Here are some clues for you:

Who swims in water
    with a group called a school?

Who has thick brown fur
    and keeps cool in a pool?

Who howls with a laugh
    and sounds like a fool?

Whose long curvy teeth
    are used as a tool?

Who speaks with a roar
    and can purr and drool?

And who did the animals see?
Mom, Dad, my brother, and me.

Take the story home. Read it to your family.

Word Family Stories and Activities • EMC 3356 • © Evan-Moor Corp.

Name_____

About "Who's Who at the Zoo"

Match the clue to the animal.

1. roars, purrs, and drools   •   • bear

2. swims in a school   •   • shark

3. laughs like a fool   •   • lion

4. cools down in a pool   •   • hyena

Fill in the circle next to the correct answer.

1. Why does a bear need a pool?

   ○ Bears like to swim.
   ○ A bear's thick fur can be hot.
   ○ Bears swim in a school.

2. What is a group of sharks called?

   ○ a pack
   ○ a school
   ○ a flock

3. Who is talking in the story?

   ○ the mom
   ○ the dad
   ○ the child

Name _____

Write **-ool** Words

Fill in the circle next to the name of the picture.

1.

○ spool
○ stool
○ school

2.

○ stoop
○ stop
○ stool

3.

○ pool
○ tool
○ cool

Complete the sentences.
Use the words below.

> fool   cool   drool   pool   stool

1. The bears swim in the _____ at the zoo.

2. My big brother likes to play jokes and _____ me.

3. Babies _____ a lot.

4. Dad sits on a _____ in his shop.

5. A fan keeps me _____ on a hot day.

Note: Cut out the slider parts along the dashed lines.
Then slip the word strip through the slider window.

Slide and Read

↑
Pull Up

cool

fool

pool

tool

drool

spool

stool

school

car pool

high school

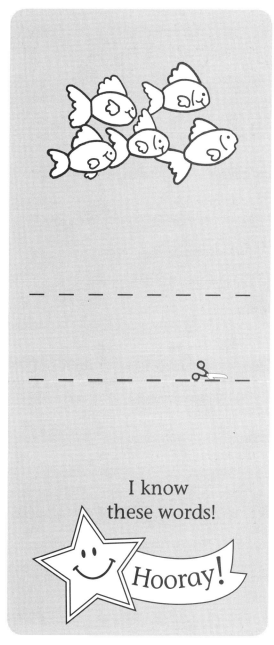

The **-ool** Family

I know
these words!

Hooray!

cool

fool

stool

tool

school

pool

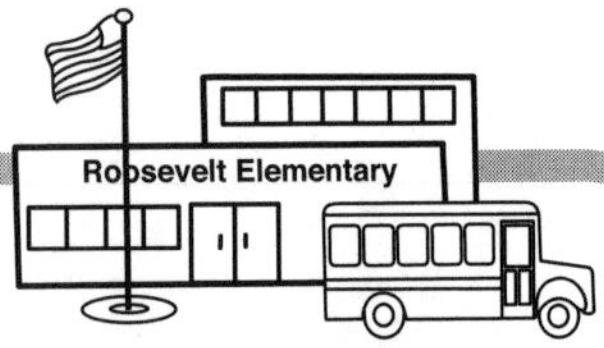

Roosevelt Elementary

end of
-ool family

car pool

cool

spool

fool

stool

drool

high school

tool

pool

Meet the **-ore** Word Family

Word Family Practice

Write the letters on the lines to make **-ore** words.
Then sound out the words you made.

1.   ch + ore   ___ ___ ___ ___ ___

2.   sc + ore   ___ ___ ___ ___ ___

3.    sh + ore   ___ ___ ___ ___

4.   sn + ore   ___ ___ ___ ___ ___

5.   st + ore   ___ ___ ___ ___ ___

Read these **-ore** words.

bore   core   wore

Complete each sentence. Use the words above.

1. My _____ at home is setting the table.

2. I think opera music is a _____.

3. My soccer team can _____ up to ten goals.

Words to know: weekly, umpire, listen
Teacher: Read the story to your students.

Word Family

-ore

Name _____

Listen as the story is read to you.
Underline the words in the **-ore** family.
Then read the story to yourself.

The Biggest Bore

Cleaning my room is such a bore!

But cleaning is my weekly chore.

I'd rather go fishing from the shore,

or be an umpire keeping score,

or try on dresses at a store,

or listen to my puppy snore.

Cleaning is the biggest bore!

I don't want to clean anymore!

Now where is the jacket I just wore?

Uh, oh!

I'd better clean my room some more.

Take the story home. Read it to your family.

About "The Biggest Bore"

Fill in the circle next to the correct answer.

1. What is the story about?

○ a messy room

○ a chore that's a bore

○ a lost jacket

2. Which of these would the girl rather do?

○ be a puppy at a store

○ be a mother mopping a floor

○ be an umpire keeping score

3. How often does the girl have to clean her room?

○ every day

○ every week

○ every month

4. How do you know that the girl is really bored?

○ She would rather listen to her puppy snore.

○ She would rather try on hats at a store.

○ She would rather go and play.

5. Where is the girl's jacket?

○ in a store

○ on the shore

○ in her room

Write **-ore** Words

Fill in the circle next to the name of the picture.

1.

   ○ school
   ○ scout
   ○ score

2.

   ○ chore
   ○ store
   ○ sore

3.

   ○ champ
   ○ core
   ○ chore

Complete the sentences.
Use the words below.

> bore   more   shore   store   tore

1. Please buy some rice at the _____.

2. The kitten _____ my shirt and made a hole.

3. We picked shells along the _____.

4. Would you like some _____ carrots?

5. Playing the same game over and over is a _____.

Note: Cut out the slider parts along the dashed lines.
Then slip the word strip through the slider window.

Slide and Read

↑
Pull Up

bore

core

more

sore

tore

wore

chore

score

shore

snore

store

The **-ore** Family

I know
these words!

Hooray!

bore

core

more

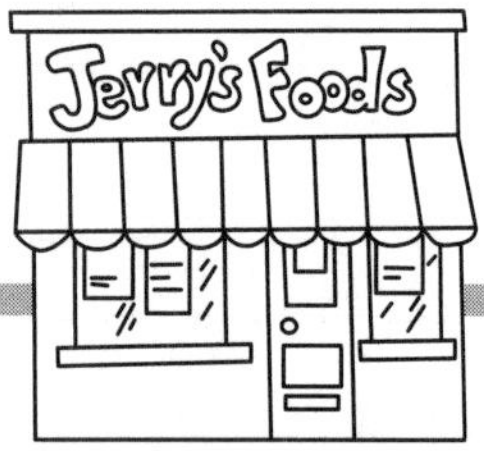

score

store

sore

end of
-ore family

shore

chore

tore

bore

snore

wore

store

chore

sore

Name _____

Meet the **-ound** Word Family

Word Family Practice

Write the letters on the lines to make **-ound** words.
Then sound out the words you made.

1.  b + ound   ___ ___ ___ ___ ___

2.  f + ound   ___ ___ ___ ___ ___

3. 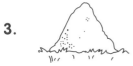 m + ound   ___ ___ ___ ___ ___

4. p + ound   ___ ___ ___ ___ ___

5. gr + ound   ___ ___ ___ ___ ___ ___

Read these **-ound** words.

hound   round   sound

Complete each sentence. Use the words above.

1. My dirty clothes formed a _____ in my room.

2. My puppy likes to _____ onto my lap.

3. The wind made a soft _____.

Words to know: below, slid, flash, licked, laughed
Teacher: Read the story to your students.

Name _____

Listen as the story is read to you.
Underline the words in the **-ound** family.
Then read the story to yourself.

A Mound on the Ground

Jada and I sat at the top of the slide.

"What's that sound?" Jada asked.

There was a soft pound.

"I hear it, too!" I said.

We looked around.

The sound came from the sand below.

We saw a mound on the ground.

Then we saw the mound on the ground move!

"Get it!" cried Jada.

We slid down in a flash.

The mound bounded into my lap.

It was a dog!

He licked Jada's face.

"We found a pet!" I said.

"So you were the mound on the ground!" laughed Jada.

Word Family Stories and Activities • EMC 3356 • © Evan-Moor Corp.

Name _____

 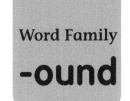
About "A Mound on the Ground"

Fill in the circle next to the correct answer.

1. What is the story about?

  ○ going to a pet store
  ○ finding a dog
  ○ playing on a mound

2. Where does the story take place?

  ○ at a park
  ○ at a store
  ○ in a pool

3. Why did the mound move?

  ○ The mound was kicked.
  ○ The wind blew it.
  ○ The mound was a dog.

4. Where was the sound?

  ○ on top of the slide
  ○ on the swing
  ○ at the bottom of the slide

5. How do you know the dog was happy to see Jada?

  ○ The dog made a sound.
  ○ The dog licked Jada's face.
  ○ The dog sat in Jada's lap.

Name _____

Write **-ound** Words

Complete the sentences.
Use the words below.

> around   ground   pound   round   sound

1. The car's horn made a silly _____.

2. I heard the rain _____ on the roof.

3. The Earth is _____.

4. We turned _____ and walked back home.

5. Some animals dig holes and live under the _____.

Write a sentence about a day at a park. Use the word **found**.

_____

_____ .

Write a sentence about a scary time. Use the word **sound**.

_____

_____ .

Note: Cut out the slider parts along the dashed lines.
Then slip the word strip through the slider window.

Slide and Read

↑

Pull Up

bound

found

hound

mound

pound

round

sound

around

ground

playground

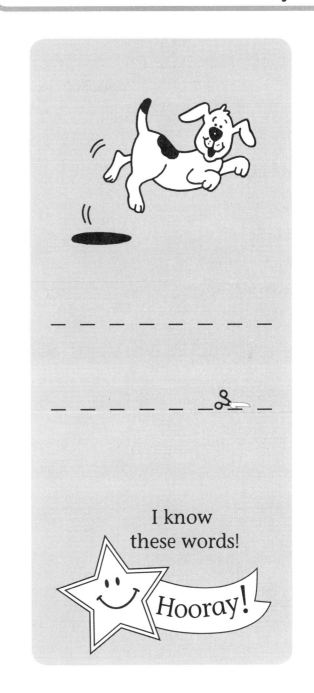

The **-ound** Family

I know
these words!

Hooray!

bound

found

hound

mound

round

ground

end of
-ound family

sound

bound

hound

found

mound

around

playground

pound

ground

Meet the -own Word Family

Word Family Practice

Write the letters on the lines to make -**own** words.
Then sound out the words you made.

1.   d + own   __ __ __ __

2.   g + own   __ __ __ __

3.    t + own   __ __ __ __

4.   cl + own   __ __ __ __ __

5.    cr + own   __ __ __ __ __

6.   fr + own   __ __ __ __ __

Complete each sentence. Use the words above.

1. The king wears a _____ of gold on his head.

2. A _____ is a smile turned upside down.

3. The _____ wore a bright red wig.

Name _____

Listen as the story is read to you.
Underline the words in the **-own** family.
Then read the story to yourself.

The Clown with a Frown

Sammy the clown's mouth turned down.

"We'll fix your frown," said the kids in town.

Katie turned upside down.

Mazy danced in a shiny gown.

Lee wore a marshmallow crown.

Rocky juggled balls of brown.

But the frown stayed down.

Then Mazy gave the clown a lick.

Rocky sat on his knee.

Katie and Lee said, "We'll be your friend."

Sammy was as happy as can be!

No more frown for Sammy the clown.

Take the story home. Read it to your family.

Name _____

About "The Clown with a Frown"

Circle one sentence in Beginning, Middle, and End to retell the story.

Beginning

1. Sammy the clown frowns.

2. Sammy is happy.

3. Mazy dances.

Middle

1. Kids and pets try to make Sammy frown.

2. Kids and pets try to make Sammy smile.

3. Sammy juggles brown balls.

End

1. Sammy the clown frowns.

2. Lee wears a crown.

3. Sammy the clown smiles.

Why does Sammy smile at the end of the story?

○ a dancing cat is funny

○ because a marshmallow crown is silly

○ because the kids said they would be his friend

Draw a line to make a match.

1. Lee wore a crown.   •   •

2. Mazy wore a gown.   •   •

3. Katie turned upside down.   •   •

4. Sammy had a frown.   •   •

Name_____

Write **-own** Words

Write the name of each picture.

1. _____ 2. _____ 3. _____

Complete the sentences.
Use the words below.

> brown   down   gown   frown   town

1. Rosa's dog has long _____ fur.

2. Some train tracks run through my _____.

3. The stairs go _____ to the subway.

4. Ola wore a pretty _____ to the dance.

5. Tom was sad and wore a _____.

Note: Cut out the slider parts along the dashed lines.
Then slip the word strip through the slider window.

Slide and Read

Pull Up

down

gown

town

brown

clown

crown

drown

frown

upside down

The **-own** Family

I know
these words!

Hooray!

gown

down

brown

clown

crown

town

end of
-own family

drown

down

crown

gown

brown

frown

upside down

clown

town

Name_____

Meet the -ue Word Family

Word Family Practice

Write the letters on the lines to make -**ue** words.
Then sound out the words you made.

1.   bl + ue   ___ ___ ___ ___

2.    cl + ue   ___ ___ ___ ___

3.   gl + ue   ___ ___ ___ ___

Read these -**ue** words.

cue   hue   true   due

Complete each sentence. Use the words above.

1. Juan used _____ to stick the picture on the paper.

2. I did not lie. What I told you is _____.

3. Give me a hint, or a _____.

Words to know: believe, month, homework
Teacher: Read the story to your students.

Word Family

-ue

Name _____

Listen as the story is read to you.
Underline the words in the **-ue** family.
Then read the story to yourself.

A Very Bad Day!

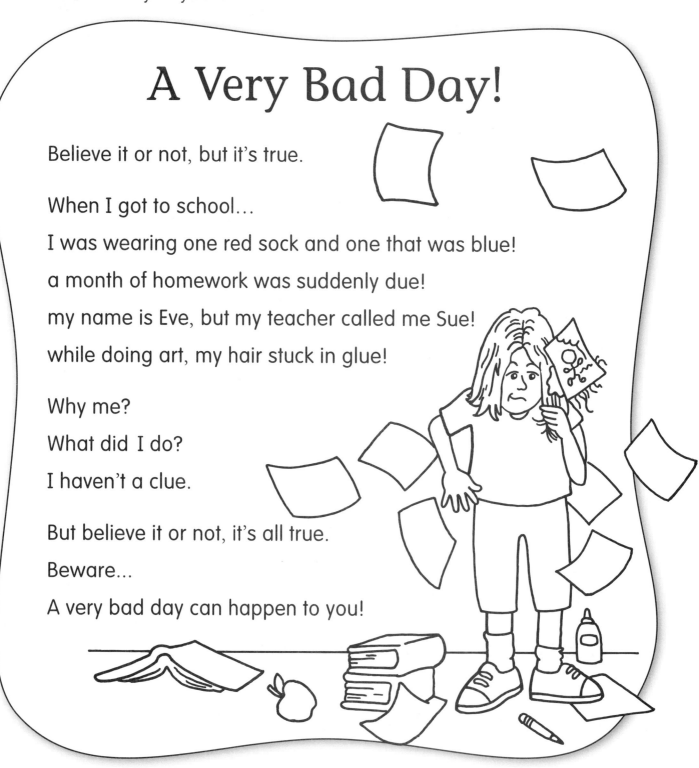

Believe it or not, but it's true.

When I got to school…

I was wearing one red sock and one that was blue!

a month of homework was suddenly due!

my name is Eve, but my teacher called me Sue!

while doing art, my hair stuck in glue!

Why me?

What did I do?

I haven't a clue.

But believe it or not, it's all true.

Beware…

A very bad day can happen to you!

Take the story home. Read it to your family.

About "A Very Bad Day"

Fill in the circle next to the correct answer.

1. Eve is telling the story.

○ yes

○ no

2. The girl's socks did not match.

○ yes

○ no

3. The girl's hair stuck to peanut butter.

○ yes

○ no

4. The girl had a good day at school.

○ yes

○ no

5. The girl knew why things were bad that day.

○ yes

○ no

6. The word **beware** probably means "watch out."

○ yes

○ no

Name_____

Write **-ue** Words

Fill in the circle next to the name of the picture.

1.

2.

3.

1.
- ○ blew
- ○ blue
- ○ boo

2.
- ○ clue
- ○ glow
- ○ glue

3.
- ○ Sue
- ○ teacher
- ○ Eve

Complete the sentences.
Use the words below.

> clue   due   glue   blue   true

1. Is that story _____?

2. Megan needed a _____ to answer the puzzle.

3. When is our homework _____?

4. David used _____ to fix the frame.

5. The sky was a reddish _____ color.

Word Family Stories and Activities • EMC 3356 • © Evan-Moor Corp.

Note: Cut out the slider parts along the dashed lines.
    Then slip the word strip through the slider window.

Slide and Read

↑
Pull Up

cue

due

hue

Sue

blue

clue

glue

true

untrue

overdue

The -ue Family

I know
these words!

Hooray!

cue

hue

due

overdue

Sue

hue

**end of
-ue family**

clue

cue

blue

due

Sue

glue

true

clue

untrue

Name _____

Word Family

-udge

Meet the **-udge** Word Family

Word Family Practice

Write the letters on the lines to make -**udge** words.
Then sound out the words you made.

1. f + udge ___ ___ ___ ___ ___

2.  j + udge ___ ___ ___ ___

3.  n + udge ___ ___ ___ ___ ___

4. sm + udge ___ ___ ___ ___ ___ ___ ___

Read these -**udge** words.

budge   grudge   sludge

Complete each sentence. Use the words above.

1. We tried to move the heavy stone, but it would not _____.

2. Sari wiped the _____ of frosting off her shirt.

3. Tony has a _____ against me because I won the race.

Words to know: battle, bellies, sharp
Teacher: Read the story to your students.

Name _____

Listen as the story is read to you.
Underline the words in the **-udge** family.
Then read the story to yourself.

The Fudge Judge

Lacey and Cory could hardly budge.

The battle of the bellies was over.

Who had eaten the most fudge?

Cory gave Lacey a sharp nudge.

There were only two pieces left.

How did they eat so much fudge?

Their eyes went to the judge.

What was that on his shirt?

It was a smudge.

It was a smudge of fudge!

The judge ate some fudge?

No one could hold a grudge.

After all, everyone loves fudge.

Take the story home. Read it to your family.

94   Word Family Stories and Activities • EMC 3356 • © Evan-Moor Corp.

Name _____

About "The Fudge Judge"

Fill in the circle next to the correct answer.

1. What kind of contest were Lacey and Cory in?

   ○ a fudge-eating contest
   ○ a fudge-baking contest
   ○ a smudge contest

2. Why could Lacey and Cory hardly budge?

   ○ Lacey and Cory were sleepy.
   ○ Lacey and Cory were full from the fudge.
   ○ Lacey and Cory stood up for the judge.

3. What does "the battle of the bellies" describe?

   ○ a stomach fight
   ○ a fat judge
   ○ an eating contest

4. How do you know that the judge ate some fudge?

   ○ The judge said so.
   ○ The judge had a smudge on his face.
   ○ The judge had a smudge on his shirt.

5. Why couldn't anyone hold a grudge against the judge?

   ○ because he was a fudge judge
   ○ because everyone likes fudge
   ○ because no one likes fudge

Name _____

Write -udge Words

Complete the sentences.
Use the words below.

> budge   judge   nudge   smudge

1. Mike gave Mel a _____ to get him to move.

2. Anna did not want to _____ from her place in line.

3. Emma has a _____ of paint on her jeans.

4. Mr. Lee will _____ the art contest.

Write a sentence about a contest. Use the word **judge**.

_____

_____ .

Write two things that are hard to **budge**.

_____   _____

What can make a **smudge**?

_____

Word Family Stories and Activities • EMC 3356 • © Evan-Moor Corp.

Note: Cut out the slider parts along the dashed lines.
Then slip the word strip through the slider window.

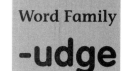

Word Family
-udge

Slide and Read

Pull Up

budge

fudge

judge

nudge

grudge

sludge

smudge

trudge

The **-udge** Family

I know
these words!

Hooray!

EMC 3356 • © Evan-Moor Corp.

Word Family Stories and Activities • EMC 3356 • © Evan-Moor Corp.

budge

judge

nudge

grudge

sludge

fudge

end of
-udge family

smudge

budge

nudge

fudge

grudge

trudge

smudge

sludge

judge

Answer Key

Page 3

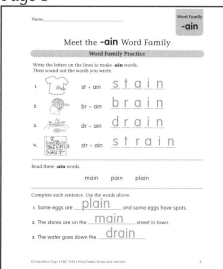

Page 4

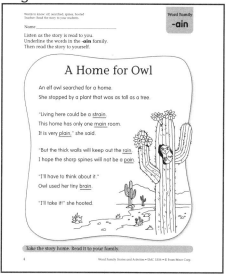

Page 5

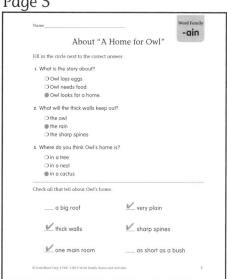

Page 6

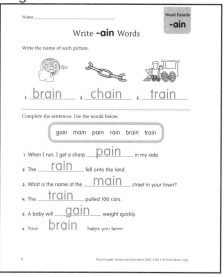

Page 9

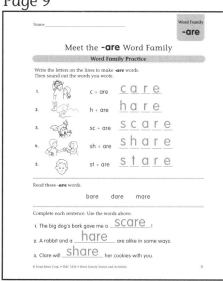

Page 10

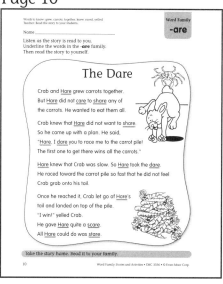

Page 11

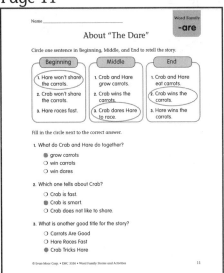

Page 12

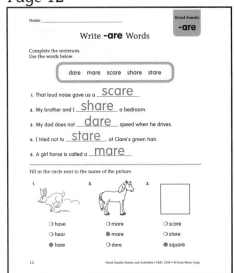

Page 15

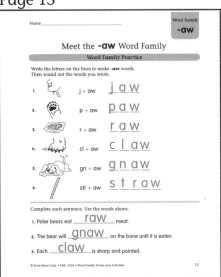

Page 16

Page 17

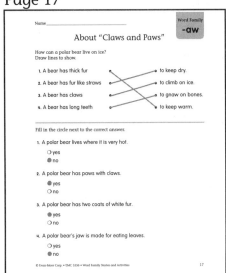

Page 18

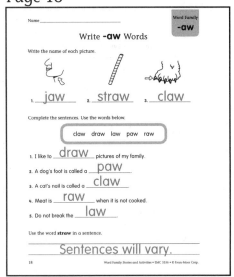

Page 21

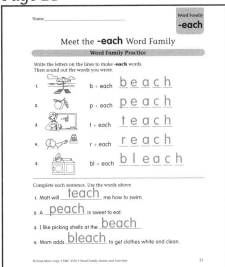

Name_____

Word Family -each

Meet the **-each** Word Family

Word Family Practice

Write the letters on the lines to make **-each** words.
Then sound out the words you wrote.

1. b + each b e a c h
2. p + each p e a c h
3. t + each t e a c h
4. r + each r e a c h
5. bl + each b l e a c h

Complete each sentence. Use the words above.

1. Matt will __teach__ me how to swim.
2. A __peach__ is sweet to eat.
3. I like picking shells at the __beach__.
4. Mom adds __bleach__ to get clothes white and clean.

© Evan-Moor Corp. • EMC 3356 • Word Family Stories and Activities   21

Page 22

Words to know: jacket, pocket, stink, empty
Teacher: Read the story to your students.

Name_____

Word Family -each

Listen as the story is read to you.
Underline the words in the **-each** family.
Then read the story to yourself.

Reach Inside

My jacket has a great big pocket.
It's easy to <u>reach</u> inside.
Last week I put in...

a soft <u>peach</u>,
a dead bug,
and shells from the <u>beach</u>.

I left the jacket on my floor all week.
The jacket began to stink.
The pocket was an icky-sticky mess!

"Let's get the <u>bleach</u> and soap," said Mom.
"I'll <u>teach</u> you how to wash your jacket."

Now I keep my pocket full during the day
and empty at night!

Take the story home. Read it to your family.

22   Word Family Stories and Activities • EMC 3356 • © Evan-Moor Corp.

Page 23

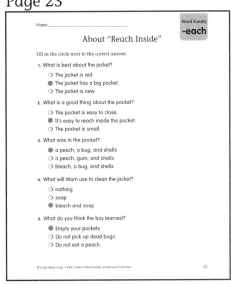

Name_____

Word Family -each

About "Reach Inside"

Fill in the circle next to the correct answer.

1. What is best about the jacket?
   ○ The jacket is red.
   ● The jacket has a big pocket.
   ○ The jacket is new.

2. What is a good thing about the pocket?
   ○ The pocket is easy to close.
   ● It's easy to reach inside the pocket.
   ○ The pocket is small.

3. What was in the pocket?
   ● a peach, a bug, and shells
   ○ a peach, gum, and shells
   ○ bleach, a bug, and shells

4. What will Mom use to clean the jacket?
   ○ nothing
   ○ soap
   ● bleach and soap

5. What do you think the boy learned?
   ● Empty your pockets.
   ○ Do not pick up dead bugs.
   ○ Do not eat a peach.

© Evan-Moor Corp. • EMC 3356 • Word Family Stories and Activities   23

Page 24

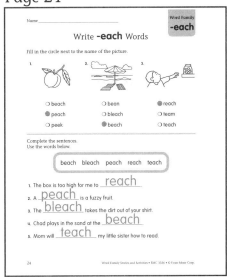

Name_____

Word Family -each

Write **-each** Words

Fill in the circle next to the name of the picture.

1. ○ beach ● peach ○ peek
2. ○ bean ○ bleach ● beach
3. ● reach ○ team ○ teach

Complete the sentences.
Use the words below.

beach   bleach   peach   reach   teach

1. The box is too high for me to __reach__.
2. A __peach__ is a fuzzy fruit.
3. The __bleach__ takes the dirt out of your shirt.
4. Chad plays in the sand at the __beach__.
5. Mom will __teach__ my little sister how to read.

24   Word Family Stories and Activities • EMC 3356 • © Evan-Moor Corp.

Page 27

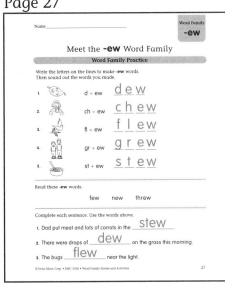

Name_____

Word Family -ew

Meet the **-ew** Word Family

Word Family Practice

Write the letters on the lines to make **-ew** words.
Then sound out the words you made.

1. d + ew d e w
2. ch + ew c h e w
3. fl + ew f l e w
4. gr + ew g r e w
5. st + ew s t e w

Read these **-ew** words.

few   new   threw

Complete each sentence. Use the words above.

1. Dad put meat and lots of carrots in the __stew__.
2. There were drops of __dew__ on the grass this morning.
3. The bugs __flew__ near the light.

© Evan-Moor Corp. • EMC 3356 • Word Family Stories and Activities   27

Page 28

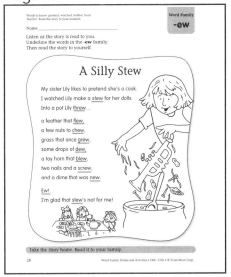

Words to know: pretend, watched, feather, horn
Teacher: Read the story to your students.

Name_____

Word Family -ew

Listen as the story is read to you.
Underline the words in the **-ew** family.
Then read the story to yourself.

A Silly Stew

My sister Lily likes to pretend she's a cook.
I watched Lily make a <u>stew</u> for her dolls.
Into a pot Lily <u>threw</u>...

a feather that <u>flew</u>,
a few nuts to <u>chew</u>,
grass that once <u>grew</u>,
some drops of <u>dew</u>,
a toy horn that <u>blew</u>,
two nails and a <u>screw</u>,
and a dime that was <u>new</u>.

<u>Ew</u>!
I'm glad that <u>stew</u>'s not for me!

Take the story home. Read it to your family.

28   Word Family Stories and Activities • EMC 3356 • © Evan-Moor Corp.

Page 29

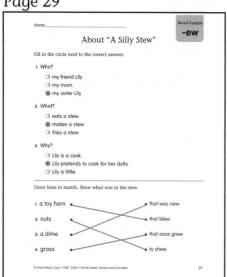

Name_____

Word Family
-ew

About "A Silly Stew"

Fill in the circle next to the correct answer.

1. Who?
   ○ my friend Lily
   ○ my mom
   ● my sister Lily

2. What?
   ○ eats a stew
   ● makes a stew
   ○ fries a stew

3. Why?
   ○ Lily is a cook.
   ● Lily pretends to cook for her dolls.
   ○ Lily is little.

Draw lines to match. Show what was in the stew.

1. a toy horn   that was new
2. nuts   that blew
3. a dime   that once grew
4. grass   to chew

© Evan-Moor Corp. • EMC 3356 • Word Family Stories and Activities   29

Page 30

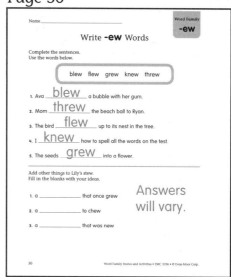

Name_____

Word Family
-ew

Write -ew Words

Complete the sentences.
Use the words below.

blew   flew   grew   knew   threw

1. Ava _blew_ a bubble with her gum.
2. Mom _threw_ the beach ball to Ryan.
3. The bird _flew_ up to its nest in the tree.
4. I _knew_ how to spell all the words on the test.
5. The seeds _grew_ into a flower.

Add other things to Lily's stew.
Fill in the blanks with your ideas.

1. a _____ that once grew
2. a _____ to chew
3. a _____ that was new

Answers
will vary.

30   Word Family Stories and Activities • EMC 3356 • © Evan-Moor Corp.

Page 33

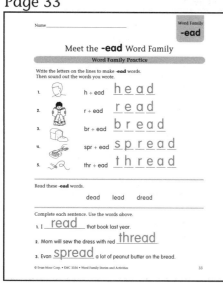

Name_____

Word Family
-ead

Meet the -ead Word Family

Word Family Practice

Write the letters on the lines to make -ead words.
Then sound out the words you wrote.

1. h + ead   _head_
2. r + ead   _read_
3. br + ead   _bread_
4. spr + ead   _spread_
5. thr + ead   _thread_

Read these -ead words.

dead   lead   dread

Complete each sentence. Use the words above.

1. I _read_ that book last year.
2. Mom will sew the dress with red _thread_.
3. Evan _spread_ a lot of peanut butter on the bread.

© Evan-Moor Corp. • EMC 3356 • Word Family Stories and Activities   33

Page 34

Words to know: peanut butter, pretend, raisins, cheese, banana
Teacher: Read the story to your students.

Word Family
-ead

Name_____

Listen as the story is read to you.
Underline the words in the -ead family.
Then read the story to yourself.

Food Face

I read this idea in a cookbook for kids.
It is called "Food Face." Here's how it goes:

You can make your face and eat it, too.
First, take one slice of bread.
Then, spread it with peanut butter.
Pretend that the bread is a head.

Make eyes with raisins.
Make a smile with jam.
Pull cheese into strings as thin as thread.
Use the strings to shape hair.
Cut the tip of a banana to form a nose.

Now go ahead and eat your face.
You will taste good!

Take the story home. Read it to your family.

34   Word Family Stories and Activities • EMC 3356 • © Evan-Moor Corp.

Page 35

Name_____

Word Family
-ead

About "Food Face"

Fill in the circle next to the correct answer.

1. Where did the food face idea come from?
   ○ It was read in school.
   ○ It was read in a funny book.
   ● It was read in a cookbook for kids.

2. What is spread on the bread?
   ○ butter
   ● peanut butter
   ○ jam

3. What do you pretend about the bread?
   ● The bread is a head.
   ○ The bread is a bed.
   ○ The bread is a sled.

4. What do you make with strings of cheese?
   ○ big eyes
   ● hair on the head
   ○ thin thread

5. What is the last thing you do?
   ○ use strings to shape hair
   ○ make eyes with raisins
   ● eat your face

© Evan-Moor Corp. • EMC 3356 • Word Family Stories and Activities   35

Page 36

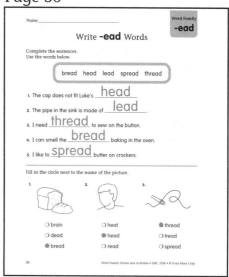

Name_____

Word Family
-ead

Write -ead Words

Complete the sentences.
Use the words below.

bread   head   lead   spread   thread

1. The cap does not fit Luke's _head_.
2. The pipe in the sink is made of _lead_.
3. I need _thread_ to sew on the button.
4. I can smell the _bread_ baking in the oven.
5. I like to _spread_ butter on crackers.

Fill in the circle next to the name of the picture.

1.
   ○ brain
   ○ dead
   ● bread

2.
   ○ heat
   ● head
   ○ read

3.
   ● thread
   ○ tread
   ○ spread

36   Word Family Stories and Activities • EMC 3356 • © Evan-Moor Corp.

Page 39

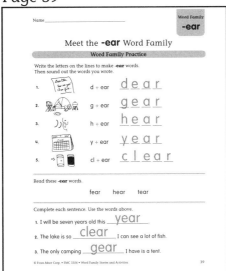

Page 40

Page 41

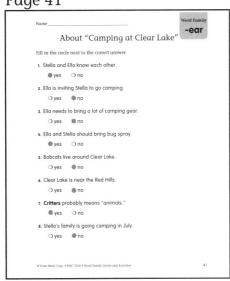

Page 42

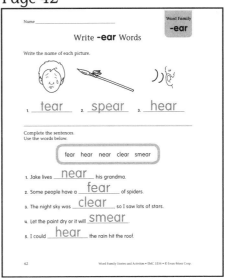

Page 45

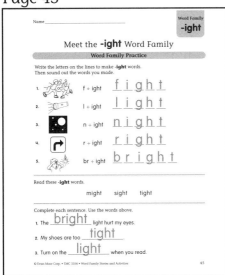

Page 46

Page 47

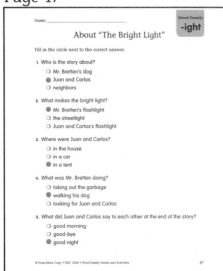

Word Family -ight

Name_____

About "The Bright Light"

Fill in the circle next to the correct answer.

1. Who is the story about?
   ○ Mr. Bretten's dog
   ● Juan and Carlos
   ○ neighbors

2. What makes the bright light?
   ● Mr. Bretten's flashlight
   ○ the streetlight
   ○ Juan and Carlos's flashlight

3. Where were Juan and Carlos?
   ○ in the house
   ○ in a car
   ● in a tent

4. What was Mr. Bretten doing?
   ○ taking out the garbage
   ● walking his dog
   ○ looking for Juan and Carlos

5. What did Juan and Carlos say to each other at the end of the story?
   ○ good morning
   ○ good-bye
   ● good night

Page 48

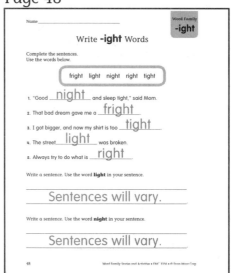

Word Family -ight

Name_____

Write **-ight** Words

Complete the sentences.
Use the words below.

fright   light   night   right   tight

1. "Good ___night___ and sleep tight," said Mom.

2. That bad dream gave me a ___fright___.

3. I got bigger, and now my shirt is too ___tight___.

4. The street ___light___ was broken.

5. Always try to do what is ___right___.

Write a sentence. Use the word **light** in your sentence.

___Sentences will vary.___

Write a sentence. Use the word **night** in your sentence.

___Sentences will vary.___

Page 51

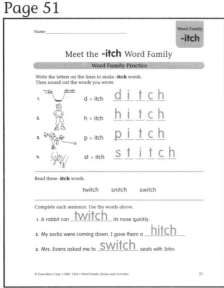

Word Family -itch

Name_____

Meet the **-itch** Word Family

Word Family Practice

Write the letters on the lines to make **-itch** words.
Then sound out the words you wrote.

1. d + itch   d i t c h
2. h + itch   h i t c h
3. p + itch   p i t c h
4. st + itch   s t i t c h

Read these **-itch** words.

twitch   snitch   switch

Complete each sentence. Use the words above.

1. A rabbit can ___twitch___ its nose quickly.

2. My socks were coming down. I gave them a ___hitch___.

3. Mrs. Evans asked me to ___switch___ seats with John.

Page 52

Word Family -itch

Words to know: ready, plate, smack, slides
Teacher: Read the story to your students.

Name_____

Listen as the story is read to you.
Underline the words in the **-itch** family.
Then read the story to yourself.

The First Pitch

It's Joy's turn to hit.
First, she stops to switch bats.
Then, she gives her pants a hitch.
She must be ready for the first pitch.

Joy steps to the plate.
Her arm gives a bit of a twitch.
Now she is ready for the first pitch.

Here it comes.
Smack! Wow!
Joy runs to first base, second base, and third.
She slides right into home plate.

Joy hit that first pitch just great!

Take the story home. Read it to your family.

Page 53

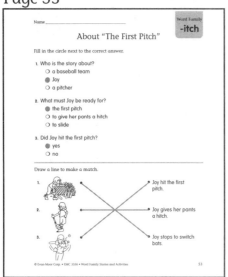

Word Family -itch

Name_____

About "The First Pitch"

Fill in the circle next to the correct answer.

1. Who is the story about?
   ○ a baseball team
   ● Joy
   ○ a pitcher

2. What must Joy be ready for?
   ● the first pitch
   ○ to give her pants a hitch
   ○ to slide

3. Did Joy hit the first pitch?
   ● yes
   ○ no

Draw a line to make a match.

1. → Joy hit the first pitch.
2. → Joy gives her pants a hitch.
3. → Joy stops to switch bats.

Page 54

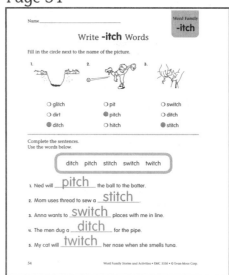

Word Family -itch

Name_____

Write **-itch** Words

Fill in the circle next to the name of the picture.

1.   2.   3.

○ glitch   ○ pit   ○ switch
○ dirt   ● pitch   ○ ditch
● ditch   ○ hitch   ● stitch

Complete the sentences.
Use the words below.

ditch   pitch   stitch   switch   twitch

1. Ned will ___pitch___ the ball to the batter.

2. Mom uses thread to sew a ___stitch___.

3. Anna wants to ___switch___ places with me in line.

4. The men dug a ___ditch___ for the pipe.

5. My cat will ___twitch___ her nose when she smells tuna.

Page 57

Name _____

Word Family -ook

Meet the **-ook** Word Family

Word Family Practice

Write the letters on the lines to make -ook words.
Then sound out the words you made.

1. b + ook — b o o k
2. c + ook — c o o k
3. h + ook — h o o k
4. l + ook — l o o k
5. t + ook — t o o k
6. sh + ook — s h o o k

Complete each sentence. Use the words above.

1. I hang my towel on a **hook** by the tub.
2. The men **shook** hands when they met.
3. The **cook** made a pot of chicken stew.

© Evan-Moor Corp. • EMC 3356 • Word Family Stories and Activities   57

Page 58

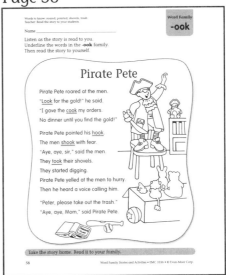

Words to know: roared, pointed, shovels, trash
Teacher: Read the story to your students.

Name _____

Word Family -ook

Listen as the story is read to you.
Underline the words in the -ook family.
Then read the story to yourself.

Pirate Pete

Pirate Pete roared at the men.
"Look for the gold!" he said.
"I gave the cook my orders.
No dinner until you find the gold!"

Pirate Pete pointed his hook.
The men shook with fear.
"Aye, aye, sir," said the men.
They took their shovels.
They started digging.
Pirate Pete yelled at the men to hurry.
Then he heard a voice calling him.

"Peter, please take out the trash."
"Aye, aye, Mom," said Pirate Pete.

Take the story home. Read it to your family.

58   Word Family Stories and Activities • EMC 3356 • © Evan-Moor Corp.

Page 59

Name _____

Word Family -ook

About "Pirate Pete"

Fill in the circle next to the correct answer.

1. What is the story about?
   ○ Peter is a real pirate.
   ○ Peter will not help his mom.
   ● Peter makes believe he's a pirate.
   ○ Pirate Pete has a hook.

2. When can the cook make the food?
   ○ at night
   ○ when Pirate Pete tells him to
   ○ when the men find the water
   ● when the men find the gold

3. Aye, aye is a way to say, "_____."
   ○ No way
   ○ You do it
   ● Yes
   ○ I'll do it later

4. Which word tells that Pirate Pete spoke loudly to the men?
   ○ said
   ● roared
   ○ pointed
   ○ shook

© Evan-Moor Corp. • EMC 3356 • Word Family Stories and Activities   59

Page 60

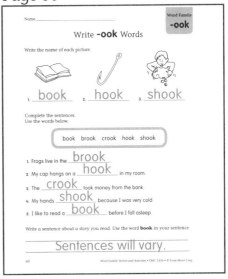

Name _____

Word Family -ook

Write **-ook** Words

Write the name of each picture.

1. book   2. hook   3. shook

Complete the sentences.
Use the words below.

| book   brook   crook   hook   shook |

1. Frogs live in the **brook**
2. My cap hangs on a **hook** in my room.
3. The **crook** took money from the bank.
4. My hands **shook** because I was very cold.
5. I like to read a **book** before I fall asleep.

Write a sentence about a story you read. Use the word **book** in your sentence.

Sentences will vary.

60   Word Family Stories and Activities • EMC 3356 • © Evan-Moor Corp.

Page 63

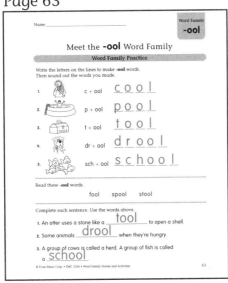

Name _____

Word Family -ool

Meet the **-ool** Word Family

Word Family Practice

Write the letters on the lines to make -ool words.
Then sound out the words you made.

1. c + ool — c o o l
2. p + ool — p o o l
3. t + ool — t o o l
4. dr + ool — d r o o l
5. sch + ool — s c h o o l

Read these -ool words.

fool   spool   stool

Complete each sentence. Use the words above.

1. An otter uses a stone like a **tool** to open a shell.
2. Some animals **drool** when they're hungry.
3. A group of cows is called a herd. A group of fish is called a **school**

© Evan-Moor Corp. • EMC 3356 • Word Family Stories and Activities   63

Page 64

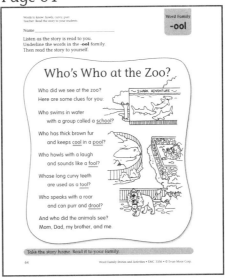

Words to know: howls, curvy, purr
Teacher: Read the story to your students.

Name _____

Word Family -ool

Listen as the story is read to you.
Underline the words in the -ool family.
Then read the story to yourself.

Who's Who at the Zoo?

Who did we see at the zoo?
Here are some clues for you:

Who swims in water
with a group called a school?

Who has thick brown fur
and keeps cool in a pool?

Who howls with a laugh
and sounds like a fool?

Whose long curvy teeth
are used as a tool?

Who speaks with a roar
and can purr and drool?

And who did the animals see?
Mom, Dad, my brother, and me.

SHARK ADVENTURE

Take the story home. Read it to your family.

64   Word Family Stories and Activities • EMC 3356 • © Evan-Moor Corp.

Page 65

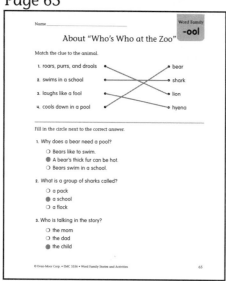

Word Family -ool

Name _____

About "Who's Who at the Zoo"

Match the clue to the animal.

1. roars, purrs, and drools •   • bear
2. swims in a school •   • shark
3. laughs like a fool •   • lion
4. cools down in a pool •   • hyena

Fill in the circle next to the correct answer.

1. Why does a bear need a pool?
   - ○ Bears like to swim.
   - ● A bear's thick fur can be hot.
   - ○ Bears swim in a school.
2. What is a group of sharks called?
   - ○ a pack
   - ● a school
   - ○ a flock
3. Who is talking in the story?
   - ○ the mom
   - ○ the dad
   - ● the child

© Evan-Moor Corp. • EMC 3356 • Word Family Stories and Activities   65

Page 66

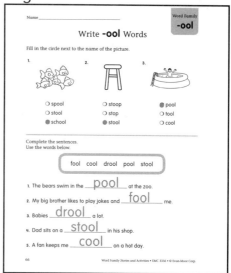

Word Family -ool

Name _____

Write **-ool** Words

Fill in the circle next to the name of the picture.

1.
   - ○ spool
   - ○ stool
   - ● school
2.
   - ○ stoop
   - ○ stop
   - ● stool
3.
   - ● pool
   - ○ tool
   - ○ cool

Complete the sentences.
Use the words below.

> fool   cool   drool   pool   stool

1. The bears swim in the ___pool___ at the zoo.
2. My big brother likes to play jokes and ___fool___ me.
3. Babies ___drool___ a lot.
4. Dad sits on a ___stool___ in his shop.
5. A fan keeps me ___cool___ on a hot day.

66   Word Family Stories and Activities • EMC 3356 • © Evan-Moor Corp.

Page 69

Word Family -ore

Name _____

Meet the **-ore** Word Family

Word Family Practice

Write the letters on the lines to make **-ore** words.
Then sound out the words you made.

1. ch + ore   _c h o r e_
2. sc + ore   _s c o r e_
3. sh + ore   _s h o r e_
4. sn + ore   _s n o r e_
5. st + ore   _s t o r e_

Read these **-ore** words.

bore   core   wore

Complete each sentence. Use the words above.

1. My ___chore___ at home is setting the table.
2. I think opera music is a ___bore___
3. My soccer team can ___score___ up to ten goals.

© Evan-Moor Corp. • EMC 3356 • Word Family Stories and Activities   69

Page 70

Words to know: weekly, umpire, listen
Teacher: Read the story to your students.

Word Family -ore

Name _____

Listen as the story is read to you.
Underline the words in the **-ore** family.
Then read the story to yourself.

The Biggest Bore

Cleaning my room is such a bore!
But cleaning is my weekly chore.

I'd rather go fishing from the shore,
or be an umpire keeping score,
or try on dresses at a store,
or listen to my puppy snore.

Cleaning is the biggest bore!
I don't want to clean anymore!

Now where is the jacket I just wore?
Uh, oh!
I'd better clean my room some more.

Take the story home. Read it to your family.

70   Word Family Stories and Activities • EMC 3356 • © Evan-Moor Corp.

Page 71

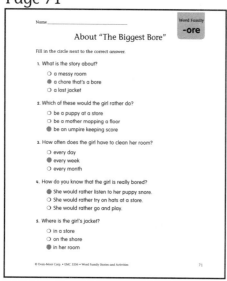

Word Family -ore

Name _____

About "The Biggest Bore"

Fill in the circle next to the correct answer.

1. What is the story about?
   - ○ a messy room
   - ● a chore that's a bore
   - ○ a lost jacket
2. Which of these would the girl rather do?
   - ○ be a puppy at a store
   - ○ be a mother mopping a floor
   - ● be an umpire keeping score
3. How often does the girl have to clean her room?
   - ○ every day
   - ● every week
   - ○ every month
4. How do you know that the girl is really bored?
   - ● She would rather listen to her puppy snore.
   - ○ She would rather try on hats at a store.
   - ○ She would rather go and play.
5. Where is the girl's jacket?
   - ○ in a store
   - ○ on the shore
   - ● in her room

© Evan-Moor Corp. • EMC 3356 • Word Family Stories and Activities   71

Page 72

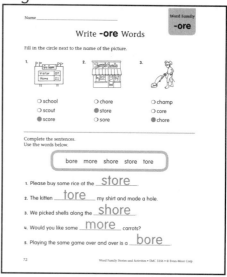

Word Family -ore

Name _____

Write **-ore** Words

Fill in the circle next to the name of the picture.

1.
   - ○ school
   - ○ scout
   - ● score
2.
   - ○ chore
   - ● store
   - ○ sore
3.
   - ○ champ
   - ○ core
   - ● chore

Complete the sentences.
Use the words below.

> bore   more   shore   store   tore

1. Please buy some rice at the ___store___
2. The kitten ___tore___ my shirt and made a hole.
3. We picked shells along the ___shore___
4. Would you like some ___more___ carrots?
5. Playing the same game over and over is a ___bore___

72   Word Family Stories and Activities • EMC 3356 • © Evan-Moor Corp.

Page 75

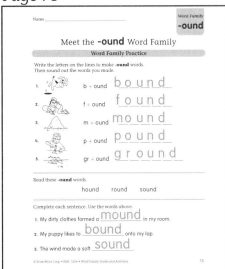

Name _____

Word Family **-ound**

Meet the **-ound** Word Family

Word Family Practice

Write the letters on the lines to make **-ound** words.
Then sound out the words you made.

1. b + ound   b o u n d
2. f + ound   f o u n d
3. m + ound   m o u n d
4. p + ound   p o u n d
5. gr + ound   g r o u n d

Read these **-ound** words.

hound   round   sound

Complete each sentence. Use the words above.

1. My dirty clothes formed a mound in my room.
2. My puppy likes to bound onto my lap.
3. The wind made a soft sound.

© Evan-Moor Corp. • EMC 3356 • Word Family Stories and Activities   75

Page 76

Words to know: below, slid, flash, licked, laughed
Teacher: Read the story to your students.

Name _____

Word Family **-ound**

Listen as the story is read to you.
Underline the words in the **-ound** family.
Then read the story to yourself.

A Mound on the Ground

Jada and I sat at the top of the slide.
"What's that sound?" Jada asked.
There was a soft pound.
"I hear it, too!" I said.

We looked around.
The sound came from the sand below.
We saw a mound on the ground.
Then we saw the mound on the ground move!
"Get it!" cried Jada.

We slid down in a flash.
The mound bounded into my lap.
It was a dog!
He licked Jada's face.
"We found a pet!" I said.
"So you were the mound on the ground!" laughed Jada.

Take the story home. Read it to your family.

76   Word Family Stories and Activities • EMC 3356 • © Evan-Moor Corp.

Page 77

Name _____

Word Family **-ound**

About "A Mound on the Ground"

Fill in the circle next to the correct answer.

1. What is the story about?
   ○ going to a pet store
   ● finding a dog
   ○ playing on a mound

2. Where does the story take place?
   ● at a park
   ○ at a store
   ○ in a pool

3. Why did the mound move?
   ○ The mound was kicked.
   ○ The wind blew it.
   ● The mound was a dog.

4. Where was the sound?
   ○ on top of the slide
   ○ on the swing
   ● at the bottom of the slide

5. How do you know the dog was happy to see Jada?
   ○ The dog made a sound.
   ● The dog licked Jada's face.
   ○ The dog sat in Jada's lap.

© Evan-Moor Corp. • EMC 3356 • Word Family Stories and Activities   77

Page 78

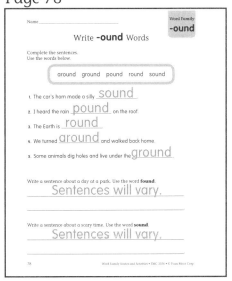

Name _____

Word Family **-ound**

Write **-ound** Words

Complete the sentences.
Use the words below.

around   ground   pound   round   sound

1. The car's horn made a silly sound.
2. I heard the rain pound on the roof.
3. The Earth is round.
4. We turned around and walked back home.
5. Some animals dig holes and live under the ground.

Write a sentence about a day at a park. Use the word **found**.

Sentences will vary.

Write a sentence about a scary time. Use the word **sound**.

Sentences will vary.

78   Word Family Stories and Activities • EMC 3356 • © Evan-Moor Corp.

Page 81

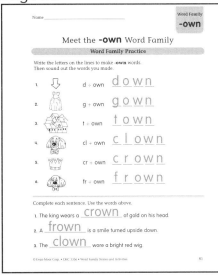

Name _____

Word Family **-own**

Meet the **-own** Word Family

Word Family Practice

Write the letters on the lines to make **-own** words.
Then sound out the words you made.

1. d + own   d o w n
2. g + own   g o w n
3. t + own   t o w n
4. cl + own   c l o w n
5. cr + own   c r o w n
6. fr + own   f r o w n

Complete each sentence. Use the words above.

1. The king wears a crown of gold on his head.
2. A frown is a smile turned upside down.
3. The clown wore a bright red wig.

© Evan-Moor Corp. • EMC 3356 • Word Family Stories and Activities   81

Page 82

Words to know: shiny, marshmallow, juggled
Teacher: Read the story to your students.

Name _____

Word Family **-own**

Listen as the story is read to you.
Underline the words in the **-own** family.
Then read the story to yourself.

The Clown with a Frown

Sammy the clown's mouth turned down.
"We'll fix your frown," said the kids in town.

Katie turned upside down.
Mazy danced in a shiny gown.
Lee wore a marshmallow crown.
Rocky juggled balls of brown.
But the frown stayed down.

Then Mazy gave the clown a lick.
Rocky sat on his knee.
Katie and Lee said, "We'll be your friend."
Sammy was as happy as can be!
No more frown for Sammy the clown.

Take the story home. Read it to your family.

82   Word Family Stories and Activities • EMC 3356 • © Evan-Moor Corp.

Page 83

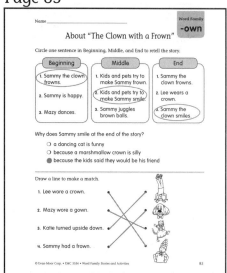

Page 84

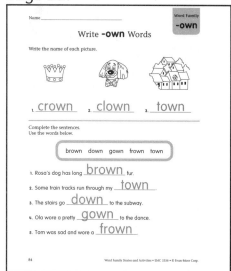

Page 87

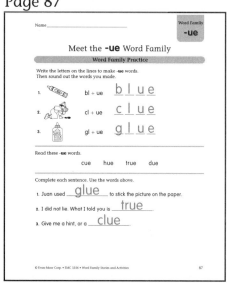

Page 88

Page 89

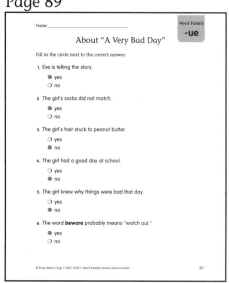

Page 90

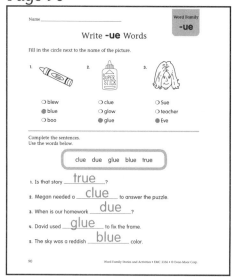

Word Family Stories and Activities • EMC 3356 • © Evan-Moor Corp.

Page 93

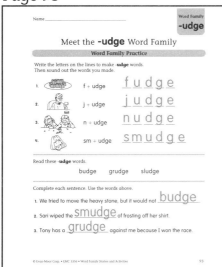

Page 94

Page 95

Page 96

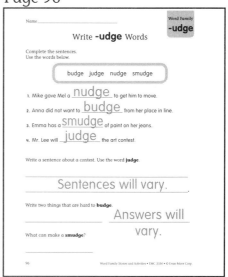

Bulletin Board

Use the train template to make a word family train for your bulletin board.

Write the word family on the engine of the train and word family words on the boxcars. Reproduce as many boxcars as needed to complete the word family your class has mastered.

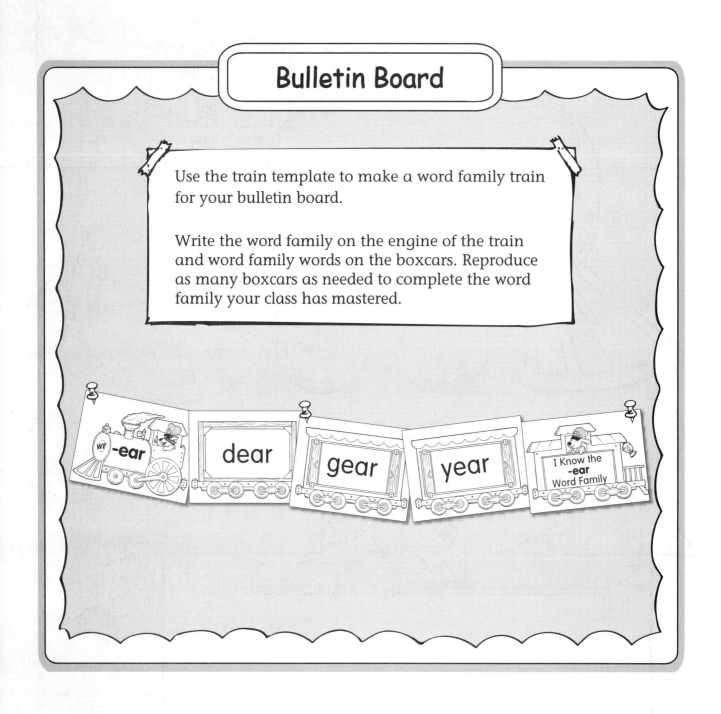

Word Family Stories and Activities • EMC 3356 • © Evan-Moor Corp.